THE CHILD AS QUEST

Method and Religious Education

J. Robert Henman

UNIVERSITY PRESS OF AMERICA

LANHAM • NEW YORK • LONDON

University Press of America,™ Inc.

4720 Boston Way
Lanham, MD 20706

3 Henrietta Street
London WC2E 8LU England

Printed in the United States of America

Library of Congress Cataloging in Publication Data

Henman, J. Robert.
The child as quest.

"Sections and chapters of this work originally appeared as a thesis for a theology degree"–Introd.
Bibliography: p.
1. Christian education–Addresses, essays, lectures. I. Title.
BV1473.H46 1983 207 83–19877
ISBN 0–8191–3633–6 (pbk. : alk. paper)

For my wife Olive, who loved me
through this entire project and
for my two children, Jay and Jill
whose desire to know inspired me on.

Robert Henman

Halifax, N.S.

August, 1983

CONTENTS

INTRODUCTION

"Wisdom leads us back to childhood. Except ye become as little children."[1]

There is an odd twist to Pascal's phrase that has a bearing on the emergence of proper catechetics. Matthew first pointed this out in his account of Jesus' reply to the disciples when they asked: "Who is of greatest importance in the Kingdom of God?" Jesus replied: "I assure you, unless you change and become like children, you will not enter the kingdom of God."[2]

Blaise Pascal mentions wisdom in the opening quotation as leading us back to childhood.[3] Pascal's view of wisdom is not our topic. His idea of wisdom is exemplified in his discussion of human knowledge, both philosophic and common sense, which I find little comfort in.

"... It is a wise ignorance which knows itself."[4] Our discussion could take us into what Pascal means by "know itself". That too, would take us too far astray from our topic and lead us into a dialectic which would only presuppose our later discussion of method. But knowing itself or oneself is the challenge I hope to set forth. The presupposition, one's own intelligent quest, knowing oneself, the wisdom of the child, is our eventual disclosure. The objective is to elaborate a method in religious education, its source being the subjectivity and intersubjectivity of the growing child. It is a wisdom that leads us back to childhood. The odd twist is the child as teacher which will be revealed slowly throughout this work. Our method is philosophic only in as much as it attempts a fundational position for teaching and learning. It is not philosophic in that traditional 'philosophy' has for the most part neglected the subject, which is the child.

I drew on Pascal's and Matthew's statements to initiate the overall thrust of this work, not in any full context that Pascal might have meant, but perhaps more in line with the authenticity Christ was aware of in the child, and in that context and upon that elaboration, will be revealed the wisdom of being like a child. Before such an elaboration can occur it will be necessary to give some history of catechetics. We shall presuppose some knowledge of historical data. We shall not presuppose the underlying intellectual thought of the time and its influence upon catechetical methodology.

In the first chapter it is worth noting the development of human consciousness, for humanity does discover the new and add to the old. The absence of quidance in such a world can cause the culture to fall into decay, unknowingly. It is not the discovery that is to be scorned, it is that discovery often moves ahead blindly creating confusion and destruction in its wake. There is often the urge 'to go back' when things appear to be getting worse. This leads to favouring theories of cyclical history which denies discovery, insight and the wonder of a child's creativity as worthwhile. The development of human consciousness is conceived empirically, always open for further discovery, advance and/or revision of the old. Historical determinism will be undermined by the emergence of ever new questions to respond to through human inquiry. Method is then the manner in which education is conceived in an ongoing context.[5]

In this event chapter one attempts to elaborate the different objectives of religious education up through the ages in a methodical context. It culminates in a 20th century cultural crisis that you and I attempt to meet head on in chapters two, three, four and five.

Sections and chapters of this work originally appeared as a thesis for a theology degree. Its purpose was the elaboration of a method that would meet the cultural crisis with solution. Its style was academically diplomatic with purpose, the purpose being somewhat obvious now calls for a more stringent mode of pursuit. The cultural crisis becomes more widespread and infiltrating as one comes to grips with deeper subjectivity, to the point that diplomacy seems to add to the problem. Therefore I have chosen to rewrite the original work with additions and a diplomacy that presupposes little or no experience of the quest this work attempts to bring to one's focus. My purpose is to present a challenge to the reader, that may be worth a life. What is it to take up the task of understanding a child? Where does one begin? I hope to set down some basic beginnings for the catechist or any reader I may have. The challenge is the reader's and the author's; mine to develop a conversation between myself and you, the reader, that will initiate some insight into the education of those infinite quests we call children.

> "Modernity's challenge, briefly, is to replace blindness and naivete by a modern symbiosis of mystery and method in the genesis of insight and human progress."[6]

I would like to thank Dr. Philip McShane for his earlier comments on the initial thrust of such a project and his later encouragement and editing of portions of this work. I am also indebted to my sister, Judy Henman, who assisted with the grammatical style and my sister-in-law, Sandra Burgoyne, who typed the manuscript. I would like to especially thank my wife for her relentless support of such a project and finally, Fr. Bernard Lonergan for the inspiration I found in much of his writings helping to initiate this effort.

J. Robert Henman, B.A., M.T.S.
Director of Religious Education
St. Peter's, Dartmouth, N.S.

CHAPTER 1

The Contemporary Problem in Historical Perspective

This short work attempts to show the emergence of a contemporary problem in religious education and goes on to propose not a technique, but a foundation which can be used to develop a method of pedagogical practice. The later chapters will spell out elements of religious reform and possible human growth on what we shall call 'an invariant basis'.[1] In this first chapter we shall outline the history of catechesis since the Council of Trent, in order to give some overview of the emergence of the comtemporary problem.

After the Council of Trent and the formation of protestant groups, catechisms for both the Protestant and Catholic churches took on the form of apologetics. They were not only to educate but to defend the faith, by providing a person of faith with answers to intimidating questions from the opposing movements.

The emphasis of catechesis from the early 17th century to the 20th century was on mastering the doctrinal content of faith.[2] That was accomplished through question and answer and some explanation of the text, followed by a brief practical application of the content or a brief exhortation of virtuous living.[3] During the 17th century the Sulpician method was developed. It was basically one of question and answer through memorization. Rewards were offered as a stimulus to do better.

The De La Salle method, which arose shortly after the Sulpician method, adopted the same style as the Sulpician method with more emphasis on memorizing and reciting. It also introduced the narrative method, as used in the Gospels, as a model for teaching children.[4]

From 1850 to 1900 the Deharbe Catechism became the main educational method of Europe. Joseph Deharbe S.J. first published his catechism in 1847. It was apologetic in nature in that it was a historical proof of revelation and the divine institution of the church. It also included discussion of the sacraments and commandments. This program, Carter tells us, was for the most part too intellectual for children.[5]

At the turn of the 20th century, religious education methodology came under the influence of the methodology of the social and natural sciences. The traditional approach was seen as deductive and abstract. The new principle was to begin with concrete things and experiences so that the learner might advance to general concepts.[6]

In the United States, at this time, John Dewey advanced the idea of activity and experience in a 5 step "how we think" process. In summary fashion, Dewey's procedure consisted of the 5 following steps: 1) begin with a felt sense of the problem, 2) formulate the problem in a conceptually clear, concise way (Dewey uses the word "intellectualize"), 3) explore the available hypotheses which have a significant bearing on the solution to the problem, 4) think in the "narrow sense" about the hypotheses, analyzing and elaborating them, and 5) bring the product of the first 4 steps to a testable form and proceed with the test. Dewey's system often had too much emphasis on activity destroying the objective. The objective was to allow children's individuality to play a part in the learning process.[7]

At this time (early 20th century) in Europe, more specifically in Germany, the Munich Method was developed. This method also proposed the active instead of the passive way of teaching and learning. Smaller classes were thought to be better than larger ones. A psychological approach was used by appealing to children with an example. The example could then be developed and related to the text of the catechism. Essentially, it was a switch from text explanation to a text development method. Similiar to the Dewey method, more participation was encouraged. Josef Goldrunner points out that insight was an important factor in the Munich Method. Insight imparts a real grasp of the content of faith. Therefore the method went beyond definition and question and answer.[8]

A belief developed in the early 20th century that children had to be taught to live in the 20th century culture as christians. The life of the 20th century christian was far different than that of the Middle Ages.[9] Therefore, the text development method was more appropriate to this goal.

In 1928, a Cathechetical Congress was held in Munich where it was decided that concrete rather than abstract languages were to be used in teaching children, and that psychological rather than logical considerations were to take precedence when teaching the youth. Along with these changes, the biblical narrative approach was also cultivated in Germany and Austria. These two countries became known in the early 20th century as the home of the catechetical movement.[10]

In the United States and Canada, the idea of the catechism being unified by a central theme, i.e. Christ, was employed. He, Christ, was now realized as the final whole, and the unifying factor of each and all lessons of catechetical instruction.

The concern for a more psychological approach in methodology in the 20th century caused the rise of many catechetical methods similar to the Munich method. Some of the more popular methods were the Eucharistic method of Dr. E. Poppe in Belgium, the Sower Scheme of Msgr. Drinkwater in England, the Fulda Plan, the Active method of Canon Quinet and the successful activities program of Dr. Maria Montessori.[11]

In North America, the Baltimore Catechism, a question and answer format, had served as the basic catechetical text for over a century. Since the changes of Vatican II in liturgy and policy have begun to be implemented, old methods of religious education have fallen by the wayside. Many schools are now employing the unit program with the Christocentric idea. Each lesson consists of a group of related subjects to be given in one or two periods. The second lesson is usually concerned with creative activities, projects, reports, dramatizations and summaries all regarded as part of the assimilative process.[12] The Come to the Father series is a current program used in Canada that attempts to use and implement some such features for teaching.[13]

Twentieth century scholars have spent much time in trying to develop new and workable methods for teaching religious education. This effort has prompted some to call for a return to content. Fr. Josef Jungmann, Carter tells us, through his book The Good Tidings and Our Profession of Faith has almost single-handedly shifted the emphasis from method to content in the catechetical method.[14] Fr. Jungmann has advocated this shift in his summary statement: "The soul of our religion is 'the message of Christ'".[15] I would not detract from Jungmann's statement of Christ's message being the soul of our religion; the problem is how does one communicate that message authentically to another human being?

Carter speaks of the advantages of trying and sticking to one method as opposed to jumping from method to method which he feels will confuse and frustrate the teacher and student.[16] Sticking to a method may make the teacher comfortable but that is no rule for certitude. There is a similarity in the emergence of a unity of content and in the structure of method used to build and grasp that unity that cannot be ignored in teaching. It is to this structure that this paper addresses itself in an effort to develop a method and show the importance of such a method in teaching religious education.

This brief history of catechetical methods reveals certain features of the different periods. The Reformation put the various denominations on their guard. Apologetics became a current theme. This held very much until the late 1800's. The emergence of the social and natural sciences brought educational methodology under the influence of their procedure. The German schools excelled in this area. In North America, the Baltimore Catechism reigned until the late 1950's and was less influenced by the social and natural sciences. It was first published in 1885 as a question and answer format.[17] It was never intended to get into the hands of the laity, but it did in vast numbers for lack of anything better.

An important shift in the approach to culture has emerged in the mid 20th century which has influenced religious education in the past 20 years. The Second Vatican Council implicitly attempted to be open to a shift from classical consciousness to empirical consciousness.[18] It has become evident in religious education that the question and answer method cannot educate the faithful. The old idea of normative culture is quickly losing its ground. Dogmatic theologicans and scripture scholars no longer see eye to eye.[19] A shift to viewing culture empirically has raised the issue of method, and theology is then conceived as an ongoing process.[20]

The changes implemented, dropped or revised the old, and often the traditional. The humanities in general have experienced a decrease in their availability especially at the university level. The social and natural sciences and commerce have taken on an upsurge in their funding and job availability. This decrease in the humanities is very much a sign of the inability to integrate current theories of knowledge in the various fields of scholarship. This gap can only be closed by a theory of cognition that underpins these areas of human experience. What is also worth noting is the cultural crisis that is present in Western (and now Eastern) society due to the lack of a singular integrated theory for all education. Today's lifestyle provides the child with a world of fast foods, alienation, rapid economy and a spreadout school system where religious experience is truncated by inadequate theoretical praxis. There arises an ambiguity in the life of the child. The child's earlier questions may be seldom addressed as meaningful and the child quickly opts for the culture that currently thrives on capital gains and technological components.[21]

It remains in the following chapters to outline the possibilities of an activity that will authentically address the child, the cultural crisis and the methodological problems of the past century.

There is at present a shortage of trained religion teachers that can address the cultural crisis with an integrated methodology. Method is often understood as the ability to use various audio-visual aids, combined with a knowledge of content and enough charisma to keep the attention of the child. These are features of any process of teaching, but underlying that process is a more fundamental activity that we shall elaborate upon in the next chapter.[22]

CHAPTER II

The Child as Religious Quest

"There is the question as expressed in words. Why is the wheel round? Behind the words there may be conceptual acts of meaning, such as 'wheel', 'round', etc.

Behind these concepts there may be insights in which one grasps how to use such words as 'wheel', 'round', etc.

But what we are trying to get at is something different. Where does the 'Why?' come from? What does it reveal or represent? Already we had occasion to speak of the psychological tension that had its release in the joy of discovery.[1] It is that tension, that drive, that desire to understand, that constitutes the primordial 'Why?'. Name it what you please, alertness of mind, intellectual curiosity, the spirit of inquiry, active intelligence, the drive to know. Under any name it remains the same and is, I trust, very familiar to you."[2]

This primordial drive Lonergan calls the pure question. It is to be found familiarily in oneself by oneself. In this chapter we will consider that primordial drive as a ground for a method of pedagogical practice.

Children who are not mentally disturbed begin to ask 'what' questions as soon as they begin to speak their native language. "What is that?" tries the patience of a parent numerous times each day. This quest begins at about two years of age and may last six months or so and then it transforms into a 'why'. Discovery of the Question raises a further question. Where does the question come from? Lonergan's reply is that the question is "that drive,that desire to understand," which brings forth the 'what' and the 'why'.

The quest of children may be treated in three manners. In the first place, it may be ignored. Secondly, responses may be in a nominalist form. Thirdly, it may be nurtured.

If the question is ignored, it may be stifled. Children find little help in their quest to understand anything and slowly withdraw from the verbal activity. Eventually they may suppress the desire itself. This is more than a stimulus-response situation: it is the unfulfillment of a desire. The authority and discipline routines of a contemporary teacher or parent hold power over children. Their way, the adult way, slowly becomes the way of the children. Children who do not follow that route may be seen as rebellious, hyper-active or overly curious.

This stifling of the verbal question resulting in some degree in the stifling of the inner desire, may also affect the creativity, bodily energy and play of children, for the pure question is about anything and everything. It will seek out new ways of playing, new schemes of images in the world of fantasy. The question as embodied, as incarnate, might be exemplified by children at the age of two, who point with their whole body while asking "what's that?". They stand on tiptoes while hips, torso, arms and head all carry the question towards the object. It would seem that if this act is so critically characteristic in children, its non-emergence, or improper nurturing could lead them away from their proper development.

The second failure of response to the question is the response of nominalism: one-word answers to a question calling for explanation of an object. An example may assist in this case. A child is walking on the sidewalk with his mother and father. The child points to a large blue thing with round features and asks: 'What is that?'. Dad quickly replies; 'That is a car.' The child is not used to verbal sounds "being what something is". The child wants to know <u>what</u> 'that' <u>is</u>. The parent has grown up in a culture that has accepted and approved such responses as valid for such questions. If the community meaning of the word 'car' is known, then <u>that is</u> what is <u>called</u> a car. But <u>it is</u> more than that. It has a function, a designer, a design, a builder, and it is made from various materials. Now, children at the age of two cannot assimilate theories on the internal combustion engine or ratios of the differential axle which are both essential areas of knowledge required for a good understanding of a car. But they can move to some suggestive description. More importantly, they can come to know that words are what objects are called and not what they are. Helen Keller, who was blind, deaf and dumb had no use of words. The names or signs for objects sensed through touch, taste or smell were communicated to Helen by a certain pattern of touches on the wrist. Helen was aware the touches were not what the things sensed were, but what they are called or referred to as. This process of development is far more time-consuming and more difficult than, "It's a car." or "Quiet, no more questions." or "Go to your room".

There is implied here a quick jump to be moral with two and three year old children but moral decisions lie on what Lonergan calls the level of rationality or judgement and it presupposes development of understanding and judgement. The child is understanding very little at this early age and the 'is' question is, as of yet, immature. Moral judgements are at least several years away according to people like Piaget and Lonergan.[3] Rather than concentrate on the impossible at the ages of two or three, time is required to respond to the questions that will assist the child toward his own capacity for intelligent and rational free choice.

This brings in the third type of response to questions. It would appear that if names are not what things are, and children are not developed enough to handle complicated explanations, then simple descriptions will have to be devised for on the spot answers.

The question may be about anything, but the subject questioning may not be able to understand such an answer to such and such a question. Why is it that the child cannot understand an explanation of the workings of the internal combustion engine? The answer to that question or the lack of instances of understanding may be many. We shall present them in question form.

'What is internal?'

'What is combustion?'

'What is a piston?'

'What is compression?'

'What is exhaust?'

'What are the laws of gas and volume?'

'What is gasoline?'

'Why use gasoline?'

'Do we need air? Why?'

'What is friction?'

'What is heat?'

'How can the engine be cooled?'

'Why did anyone make an engine?'

'Did anyone make the engine or was it always there?'

These questions only scratch the surface of the instances of understanding children may lack. The last question even raises the meaning of history, creation and Creator. It becomes quickly obvious that any adequate understanding of the internal combustion engine is greatly beyond young children. There are far too many unanswered questions. How then would one approach children if one wanted to develop their knowledge of internal combustion engines?

In the first place, the presence of interest is a major factor. Some children may find the internal combustion engine a bore. If so, their questions will quickly shift. Let us say that, in our example, the children are interested. They will not ask questions they have not heard something about. If the word piston is not part of their vocabulary they cannot ask, 'What is a piston?' If they are not presently viewing a piston, they cannot ask, 'What is that?' So previous knowledge, and past and present experiences will determine the future question. The level of ability of questions is akin to the present level of development. One does not know what the next question will be, but an approximation can be made. If the child's question is a way of developing and the teacher cannot know the next question, it is the child who must ask the question. The teacher may have to wait, but explanation of previous questions will yield further questions until all relevant questions have been asked and answered.[4]

In this way, children set the pace, not the teacher, although the teacher can present experiences such as the narrative to bring a certain question to the forefront. The main point here is that questions stand on former insights and will only be understood in the context of previous insights. If children ask what a piston is because they just heard the work 'piston' and they do not know what round, steel, compression or explosion mean; that question cannot be answered properly until these further areas are explained. At this early age description would seem to be the area a child could handle. This discussion of the question depicts it as the core of intellectual development.

The former discussion regarding the stifling of

questions addressed the psychological and intellectual side of the question. It is now appropriate to address the question as religious.

"And, above all, I am desire.

Still of what am I desirous? Of many things, and not all at once. I am a variable range of desires. If I now desire play, still I will later desire rest. If sex is my desire, still sex is not everything. And somehow I desire everything.

But what is at the root of it all? This very question reveals the root. For, only the question can encompass all. If I am incarnate quests, still the focus of these quests is Question.

Not only is our desire a personal desire to understand, it is a desire to be personally understood. It is a desire for personal intimacy, sympathy, of unlimited dimensions."[5]

Desire is for unlimitedness. We are finite beings yet the question encompasses all. It holds in incarnate tension all that one knows and all that is to be known, God. In other words, questions arise from former knowledge and seek the unknown, this is a totality, known plus unknown equals all there is to be known, i.e. God. God is the embodiment of all that is to be known. God is the ultimate to be known. This is the religious quest of child, adolescent and sdult alike. The question then is religious by its nature, and its goal, the Transcendent God.[6]

If humanity's quest is for the Transcendent, it becomes apparent that we seek the Transcendent in many areas perhaps strange to 20th century theology. Our quest directs itself to the physics of the universe, to the chemistry of all matter, to botanical structures, to the zoological aspects of the entire planet and to the inner workings of our cognitional and emotional apparatus. To determine the relevance to each level of our inquiry is not our sole purpose.[7] Let us note that the question as religious searches into areas not considered religious in contemporary theological circles, and yet the world, the universe is of God.[8] As the style of this print reveals that this work is of me, so the world reveals itself through science, art and history as of God. To neglect this is to refuse to know the intended order of our world.

The religious quest of human beings reaches out everywhere. Children are bursting in their aliveness. Teachers will have to be aware of this aliveness and its acute importance in teaching and development if they are to address children authentically. To do so, that aliveness must be part of the teacher's own constitutive meaning in a new way.

Children naturally develop a mystique about God, about the world. Bad science and poor theology can destroy this mystique and has in the past in western culture.[9] When the mystery of life is gone, the fullness of the question fades with it. Is God a mystery? Is the unlimitedness of the question imaginable? Only in glimpses, one might say. A pause here might grant a glimpse. So God is and will remain that mystery: for man knows in a succession of single instances, where as God is the one whole unrestricted act of understanding.[10] The separation of our way of existing keeps us infinitely questioners and God an infinite mystery to us.

The presence of that mystery cannot be destroyed but it can fade in a dying culture. It is part of children and their proper development. Through questions and further questions, the world opens up to children. Laurens van der Post discusses in The Dark Eye of Africa[11] this very human dimension that European society has taken away from the African and now the African suffers in a homeland that is estranged. The transition from their mythological rituals to christianity destroyed the mystery in their lives. They followed blindly and many tribes now live as a suppressed and passive people. Their insights into jungle order and survival have been replaced by European styled communities and daily jobs from eight to five with a Christian Sabbath that is foreign to their agricultural and hunting forms of prividing food.

This illustrative digression to what may be called African compactness[12] could be enlarged to show the compact presence and value of mystery in man's life. Indeed, the child could be considered as an ontogenetic instance of this phylogenetic phenomenon.[13] If that mystery in man's life is removed, it is as if God is nominally obvious. To children, nothing is obvious. Their quest is long and arduous reaching beyond the world around them. Their quest is one of deep historical resonance, for one can see the whole of humankind moving in that quest towards home. "... Each member, each group, indeed our whole host and its great pilgrimage, was only a wave in the eternal stream of human beings, of the eternal strivings of the human spirit towards the East, towards Home..."[14]

There is a call then for teachers to be open to the quest of children and of humankind, sensitive to the mysterious and yet knowledgeable of the human content. None of these areas appear as small tasks. Camus tells us it takes ten years to get an idea and just as long to make it one's own.[15]

In this chapter then, we have discussed a cognitional act - the question, prior to any content, as a pure desire for anything and everything, for God. We have then moved on to address its pedagogical implications for humankind, with children as instance and mirror. Our purpose has been to present a foundation upon which teaching and learning may progress. It sets new goals for the teaching regarding child development and teacher development. The content will be a development of the pure desire within children towards religious enrichment, psychological well-being and intellectual development.

CHAPTER III

"The Situation in Contemporary Psychology and Religious Education"

Contemporary institutions of post-secondary education turn out numerous teachers for a multiplicity of tasks in the teaching world. Society maintains university structures for training and educational purposes, as well as the hope that professorial and post-graduate research will lead to some new insights, that, upon their practical application, will benefit the society. In practice this may not be the case. Perhaps a short assessment of the underlying theories of academic research is in order.

Let us keep in mind the viewpoint developed in chapter two regarding the centrality of the nurturing of the quest as a method of development, psychologically, intellectually and religiously. The current academic manuals on such topics usually provide a methodological approach in the early chapters. One need not read too far before it becomes apparent that methodology is not just a way of doing something but it also presupposes a way of viewing the world reality. Reality is conceived in the social and natural sciences as the observable, the sensed, the 'out there'. This raises some question about the reality of question itself. Our Purpose is to discover the question as a pedagogical tool. That question is a striving to discern something about the observable, or we may use the term experience, and it reveals that all is not obvious concerning the experience. There is an intelligibility to be known by the knowing subject. The current notion of reality hinders the process of coming to grips with the importance of the question as cognitive and as pure desire because the pure desire is not experienced through sense experience. It is not observable, and if it is to be included in a field of inquiry such as psychology then there is required a shift in the notions of experience and of reality. Experience is seen in such a shift not only as sensed experiences but also as acts of consciousness. When such acts are adverted to through proper guidance, they are experienced as acts of cognition. These cognitive experiences operating on sensed experiences raise questions about the primacy of the observable in current scientific studies of humanity.

In the first place, the acts of consciousness seek intelligibility in sensed experiences just as they can seek intelligibility in themselves. Eg. What is a tree? and What is the pure desire? The first question is about visual presentations, the second question is about a conscious act. The visual presentation is not a conscious act, rather, it is a given experience that consciousness may or may not advert to. The pure desire is an act of consciousness that is given in the mind and its presence is an advertence to some experience, either sense experience or cognitive experience. It remains, that both the tree or the pure desire, are possible as directions of inquiry. Furthermore, by inquiry into the nature of questioning, experience is conceived as a component of knowing just as questioning, understanding and judging are parts of a whole structure called knowing. Experience takes on a role different from that of common sense experiences in as much as it is correctly understood through the knowing structure of human consciousness. Common sense views ordinary experiences as reality. Theoreticans, through their advertence to understand, go beyond the experience just as the quest of children goes beyond the merely seen - 'What's that?' The very structure of human consciousness seeks beyond elementary experience. Reality for the theoretic can no longer remain the observable, the experienced. The observable is a component of knowing and a component of reality. Reality's full constitution rests in the intelligible reached in the act of judgement. 'What is that?' That is a vehicle of transport developed by man that works on theories of gas, metalurgy, friction, aerodynamics, electrical theory and differential gear ratios. They all integrate to function as a whole called a car. What is in mind here is the fruit of intelligence.

Such a theory of reality points towards the need for explanation of the theoretic's procedure. The person of common sense can still function in the world, for the world of common sense is everyone's world at some time during the day. 'I am hungry.' 'I will eat.' One does not have to analyze thebiological experience of hunger, to know that eating will remove the discomfort. If one wishes to know why food removes the discomfort, a study of chemistry, biology and the human anatomy is required. One has then moved to the theoretical.

When procedure shifts from common sense to theory, as exemplified in the last paragraph, common sense must move to the background of one's procedure. The notion of reality held in common sense cannot be transferred to the theoretical. Science is striving to understand the relations between things and between laws. Scientific procedure goes beyond the data. The experiments and tests are merely more data that are the fruit of former understanding. For it is the understanding that the scientist presently has, that helps raise further questions and establishes hypotheses and experiments to test those hypotheses.

Science goes beyond common sense for specific reasons. Science is attempting to understand the data to bring the world more under its control and to develop new technology to assist humanity in the raising of the standard of living. Once humanity moves in such a direction, the notion of value arises. Scientific method as it is presently outlined in philosophy does not include value questions or judgements. Scientists are presumed to leave that to administrators, politicians, and diplomats, as if they, scientists, were granted through some extraordinary power, amnesty from such a thing. This gap of responsibility on the scientist's part, coupled with the politician's lack of knowledge of what a value judgement is, leaves man in the wake and constant threat of war, depression, pollution, crime and psychological shrinkage.

The point here is that common sense can no longer control science. Not only has science been controlled by common sense thinking, but theology suffers from the same problem of inadequate analysis of the theologian's proceedings.

"Undifferentiated consciousness (a consciousness unaware of the different levels of meaning to which it can shift, eg. common sense, theory) uses indiscriminately the procedures of common sense, and so its explanations, its self-knowledge, its religion are rudimentary."[2] (Brackets are my own.)

In their proceedings, the scientist and the theologian may be following their methods precisely, but the current view of reality as 'out there' causes an ambiguity. Such an ambiguity arises "...when an Eddington contrasts his two tables: the bulky, solid, colored desk at which he worked, and the manifold of colorless 'wavicles' so minute that the desk was mostly empty space."[3] Eddington never adverted to the two different procedures of common sense and science, nor did he notice the difference between the two tables that his understanding created for him.

This dificiency also accounts for theories on objectivity that further confuse the child's notion of reality. How does one know that is a car? I merely look. Looking and knowing then take on the characteristics of synonymous activities and objectivity rests in the amount of looks that see the same thing.

"If objectivity is a matter of elementary extroversion, then the objective interpreter has to have more tolook at than spatially ordered marks on paper; 'out there'; and the difference between an objective interpreter and one that is merely subjective is that the objective interpreter observes simply the meanings that are obviously 'out there', while the merely subjective interpreter 'reads' his own ideas 'into' statements that obviously possess quite a different meaning. But the plain fact is that there is nothing 'out there' except spatially ordered marks; to appeal to dictionaries and to grammars, to linguistic and stylistic studies, is to appeal to more marks. The proximate source of the whole experiential component in the meaning of both objective and subjective interpreters lies in their own experience; the proximate source of the whole intellectual component lies in their own insights; the proximate source of the whole reflective component lies in their own critical reflection. If the criterion of objectivity is the 'obviously out there', then there is no objective interpretation whatever; there is only gaping at ordered marks, and the only order is spatial. But if the criterion of objectivity lies in intelligent inquiry, critical reflection, and grasp of the virtually unconditioned, then the humbug about the 'out there' and the simulated indignation about 'reading into' are rather convincing evidence that one has very little notion of what objectivity is."[4]

The current views ofobjectivity and reality would seem to fall short of explaining exactly what a scientist is doing when he is doing science. This current view, regarding objectivity, might be exemplified by the following quotation.

"A measurement is objective when little or no judgement is required by the measurer; all he has to do is count or read a number."[5]

Scientists attempt to back off completely: the fact is, they do not back off at all. They must know the meaning of numbers and their relation to one another, or their counting would be similar to the response of a horse tapping his foot to a certain stimulus. The scientist in such a case is merely looking at 'spatially ordered marks on various surfaces; it remains for the scientist to determine their meaning and consequence.

Our effort in this chapter has been to point out a deficiency in the account of method given by the social and natural scientist. This deficiency is the stumbling block that keeps science from adverting to the question as an experience to be understood. The emphasis on reality as 'out there' takes all focus off 'me' as alive with questions, meaning and desires that the scientists cannot observe, and so must ignore. One can authentically ask the question, 'Am I Questioning?' and one is doing just that. The solution lies in adverting to the non-observable activity, its origin and its object.

The sublation of the cognitional act, question, to a level of awareness that can be appreciated in its full implications resides in the subject adverting seriously to himself as questioner. The failure to advert to the acts of consciousness has a long history yet there are high points in the events setting trends for possible future progress. Thomas Aquinas drew on Aristotle[6] and affirmed as a matter of experience insight into phantasm as the first part of the process that moves from sense through understanding to essential definition.[7] Duns Scotus denied the fact of insight into phantasm. Scotus posits concepts before understanding: understanding merely sees a nexus between concepts.[8] In such a system concepts take priority and the acts of intelligence take a backseat. Question, insight and judgement fail to be addressed as significant moments of intellectual endeavour. Kant affirmed that intellect was purely discursive, and that all intuition is sensible.[9] These features of developing philosophy from the 13th century up through Hume and Kant, kept the significance of questioning in philosophical discussions at a lowpoint. Hegel swung all the way to Idealism.[10] The existentialist caused a turn to human subjectivity, but they fell short of a detailed account of cognitional apparatus and epistemological problems.[11] Therefore, the rise of the social sciences in the late 19th century, influenced by scientific method and the philosophy of Kant, neglected the activity of questioning as significant in doing psychology or sociology. The work of these sciences laid the groundwork for methods in education for the 20th century that were discussed in chapter one.

The current curricula of the Bachelor of Education programs are backed by the shift Scotus originated in the late 13th century. The final year of the Education program is heavily laden with psychology courses to assist the teacher in helping the student to learn. The techniques may be under the name of experimental, developmental or behavioural psychology. Most psychology textbooks do not mention question in their indices. The question of Question never arises in the print, therefore we can assume it does not arise as a relevant issue in the mind of the author or the professor for that matter. The issue has arisen minutely in christian circles. Pierre Babin has brought attention to the question as something for further study.[12] Babin does not develop his thoughts on the matter relating to cognition or epistemology. His advertence is directly to pedagogy. But if the cognitional and epistemological relevance is missed the question remains a theoretical enterprise. Lonergan has outlined the psychological and intellectual importance of question in Insight.[13] McShane has intimated the religious aspect of any and all quests[14] revealing the development of the term 'secular' as an invalid notion of the contemporary academic scene. The question is not discussed in such a manner in neither philosophy of science courses or psychology lectures and/or manuals relating to methodology.

A student graduating with the Bachelor of Education degree is qualified to teach in most schools in North America. They graduate in large numbers each year. Security rests on the mindset of the degree-granting institution and the institution they teach in. "Imperceptibly the corruption spreads from the harsh sphere of material advantage and power to the mass media, the stylish journals, the literary movements, the educational process, the reigning philosophies. A civilization in decline digs its own grave with a relentless consistency. It cannot be argued out of its self-destructive ways, for argument has a theoretical major premise, theoretical premises are asked to conform to matters of fact, and the facts in the situation produced by decline more and more are absurdities that proceed from inattention, oversight, unreasonableness and irresponsibility."[15]

In a culture as depicted above, the question, as a relevant issue, never arises within the confines of that culture. The child is 'seen' as curious. Such a culture accepts the traditional basis of educational theories. That basis stifles and suppresses the pure desire we spoke of in chapter two; it modifies emotional and intellectual development in such a way as to orient the child to looking and naming.

If life is to become more liveable, and students of faith are to find their searching fulfilled, then a shift of educational theory is in order. It is to this shift that our attention has been focused all along. I would like to end this chapter with a further quotation regarding the problem and difficulty of the emergence of solution and shift.

"The neglected subject does not know himself. The truncated subject not only does not know himself but also is unaware of his ignorance and so, in one way or another, concludes that what he does not know does not exist."[16]

The truncation of present scholarship would appear quite massive in the light of our remarks regarding common sense and theory. My inclusion of this quotation is to show the difficulty of the emergence of the 'question' in contemporary psychology and methodology. Its emergence is blocked by the notions of reality and objectivity that stand solid in contemporary academia. If the question is blocked, then so is the emergence of an adequate analysis of human cognition. For analysis presupposes questioning about some experience: in this case, the acts of consciousness; more specifically, the congitional act of question itself.

CHAPTER IV

"Elements of Proximate Reform"

In chapter one we outlined the emergence of a problem of method in religious education and the social and natural sciences. This problem we came to see as a cause of a cultural crisis for the child growing in the world. Chapter two explored the quest of the child as pure desire and as religious. This exploration laid a groundwork for a pedagogical practice to assist in the psychological, intellectual and religious development of the child. Chapter three attempted to indicate the gaps between current scholarship, more specifically methodology in psychology, and the view offered in chapter two. In this present chapter the possibilities and schemes required for reform of the situation presented in chapter three will be discussed. If the solution offered in chapter two is to become a reality for the teacher, the problem raised in chapter III must be understood in its wider ramifications, meaning the far-reaching influences of a society controlled by common sense and truncation in a period of theoretic emergence and technological exploration.

The problem raised in chapter three leads to a cultural crisis that might be termed fragmentation.[1] Fragmentation or fragmented consciousness is the ambiguity of living that arises when an undifferentiated consciousness moves into different levels of meaning and is unable to explain the shift in meaning. If one does not know the difference between common sense, theory and interiority, one cannot authentically differentiate between the meaning of each level of meaning.

In a culture where common sense rules theoretical judgement and value, the possibility of error is increased. It is increased because common sense is not of the theoretical. It is like the blind trying to understand color. Common sense's position on reality and objectivity are restrained by the very procedure and role of common sense in human living. Theory is an emergence in the development of human consciousness beyond that of common sense. Common sense notions of reality push for a reductionism in science.[2] The procedure of science may be methodical, but the underlying premise is grounded in common sense seeking a basic 'stuff' of reality. Real induction, in contrast, is the movement from experience (data) to understanding and conclusion. It is an integrative process of scientific knowing and knowledge. Just as Eddington contrasts his two tables, the one he worked on and the one he came to know through the laws of molecular structure, in the same way, undifferentiated consciousness becomes a fragmented consciousness and the possibility of a cultural crisis emerges. If the culture is to shift to remove the incoherence between levels of meaning, fragmented consciousness must be by-passed. One must move from compact consciousness[3] to integrated consciousness.[4]

"Any realm (of meaning) becomes differentiated from the others when it develops its own language, its own distinct mode of apprehension, and its own cultural, social, or professional group speaking in that fashion and apprehending in that manner."[5]

Let us delineate further about differentiation of consciousness. The African Bushman is one of the few living examples of compact consciousness. Van der Post tells us the European world is destroying the African consciousness by the mode of thrust of the European culture on the African.[6] The Black people of Africa once felt the dangers of the deep jungle. They were totally sensitive to the botanical and zoological growth as it moved about them. That ability is gone and deaths in the jungle are more frequent. The Africans can no longer live in their own land. In their home, they are strangers.[7] The Black consciousness of 19th century Africa integrated the world which made sense of the world they strived in for their present needs. The introduction of other modes of culture without explicit sensitivity to the African consciousness brought about troubled consciousness.[8]

In this same way theory emerges in the 17th century[9] and its operators are people of common sense.[10] The inability of common sense to explain theory is not a fault of common sense. Common sense cannot explain common sense because it is a complicated structure whose explanation requires reflection on procedures of thinking and doing. Common sense does not reflect on thinking and doing. It responds to one's biological, physiological, zoological and chemical habitat. I am hungry, I will eat. If common sense cannot explain its own mode of operations, it surely cannot explain a higher development of operations: the theoretical, the scientific. It also remains that science cannot explain the workings of common sense. Science, because of its method, attempts to explain the world of sense experience. But common sense is a structure of experience, understanding, judgement and doing. Science also cannot explain its own procedures. For what the 'scientist' is doing when he is doing science, also rests on an account of the data of consciousness. The level of meaning that proceeds to an analysis of the data of consciousness, is called interiority.[11]

It is at this point, at this level of meaning that we arrive at a position that is and can be critical of common sense and theory. Such a level of meaning can give an account of both levels of meaning. An integration is achieved by the subject who comes to know himself as one who can shift from one level to another and knows when he does so.

"The unity, then, of differentiated consciousness is, not the homogeneity of undifferentiated consciousness, but the self-knowledge that understands the different realms and knows how to shift from any one to any other. It remains, however, that what is easy for differentiated consciousness appears very mysterious to undifferentiated consciousness or to troubled consciousness."[12]

Such a move to interiority for the methodologist solves the problem of fragmented consciousness to some degree.[13] It remains to have such an awareness bear its fruits in the common sense subject who does not aspire to such a manner of reflection.

If scholarship becomes a world of differentiated consciousness in the fields of science, economics, politics, history, art and religion, the culture emerges in a different context. For whatever field one is in, there is always the religious quest of the subject and the question of judgement and of value: 'Is it so?' The integration of human scholarship integrates the world for the common sense subject. Communication becomes a specialized field that does not attempt to further confuse the man in the street. This integration must also include artistry. Artistry resides on the dramatic side of the subject and is crucial to human living.[14] This may be seen in the child's world of imagination and played-out fantasies. The pressure of adult on child to be disciplined, to be seen and not heard and current educational programs are largely a stifling of their creativity. The educational systems which suppress questions will slowly drain the artistic dimension of human aliveness. On many current television educational programs, children are asked to imagine a tree or whatever and instantly a tree pops onto the screen. Children do not get a chance to imagine anything. Once the picture of a tree appears on the television screen the child stops any process of imagining that may have begun. Eventually, the ability to imagine, to associate the experience of sound, the meaning of language and the activity of creative imagination all become stifled.

Artistry is a dimension of human subjectivity and intersubjectivity that has its origins in the symbolic. "A symbol is an image of a real or imaginary object that evokes a feeling or is evoked by a feeling."[15] The child plays out day to day routines of adults with toys and re-enacts shows seen or stories told. The child lives in this world to its fullest capacity. To negate or ignore that world is to by-pass a valuable teaching tool. If artistry is not part of the community, the child grows to lose such a world. Creativity becomes the propriety of a few and the lack of artistic development prevents the subject from authentic enjoyment of the various forms of art, and psychological shrinkage pervades for lack of association towards symbolism.

Common sense has its procedure that can lead to teaching and learning, theory can assist in the process, but interiority underpins and guides both processes, but, "human knowing and feeling are incomplete without expression. The development, then, of symbols, of the arts, of a literature is intrinsic to human advance."[16]

Bruno Snell outlines such a development in his Discovery of Mind. Homeric epics drew on the characteristics of inanimate nature, plants and animals, to bring forth and make distinct the various actions of the heroes in the story.[17] It was a method of objectification. Art is objectified through the symbol that is an embodiment of the meaning that is in the consciousness of the artist. Its objectification is a revealing of meaning that unleashes the tension of meaning to be objectified - to be able to say - 'That is what I want to say.' - about whatever. The child unleashes his world in the dramatic roles he constantly plays out. It is a world of expression and discovery. The child discovers new skills he can perform, the new movements can be incorporated and integrated with old movements. The dramatic role becomes a process of learning for the child that he or she can carry on alone. They are teacher and student in one.[18]

Therefore, our discussion of the levels of meaning cannot exclude the realm of art. For just as common sense, theory and interiority are ways of coming to know different objects and subjects, so is art a way of knowing different objects and subjects. To exclude it is to cut off part of the natural development of the child. So our discussion of community now includes four levels of meaning; i.e. common sense, theory, interiority and art.

The educational institutions must, in this prior context, address the realm of common sense, theory, interiority, and art if it is to nurture the child's growth authentically. The confrontation of intersubjectivity, i.e. communal living, must be authentic so that he or she who is confronted will not become unauthentic. Joining children in their dramatic world is a joy for children. They delight in the playtime others share with them. The authentic subjectivity of the child reaches out for intimacy; they are in love with parents and friends. In so far as the parents, the community, grow in the same authenticity, a new community arises.

In the light of previous remarks,[19] teaching is now seen as guided by the child's present orientation. If the young child is in a world of play and dream, then the narrative will be one of the younger child's homes for learning. The narrative presents a whole. Earlier we spoke of the question as a drive for unity, for a whole.[20] The narrative presents itself as a possible whole and with the end of the story it becomes a complete whole. The wholeness of the child's quest is fulfilled prior to the end by the expectation of an end. That expectation is fulfilled with the ending of the story.

In order that a story get through to the child it must be presented in a way that the child understands. The child knows a world of play and make-believe, of acting out with biological movements the fantasies of imagination. The narrative must address, in its presentation, that side of the child, that 'at-homeness' with fantasy. The teacher must embody the meaning of the story and live that meaning in the presentation and in the discussion. The presentation must move to gesture, to forms of expression that constitute meaning for the listener. Just as the young child asks 'what' with his whole self,[21] so the storyteller must tell the story with their whole body, mind and heart.

The ability of a teacher to embody the narrative in such a way rests much on the aliveness of the community in which one grows. A culture void of artistry and symbolic gesture and expression will bring forth few dramatic personalities. Art becomes a privilege of the few. The culture that addresses the child authentically nurtures the subject to authentic subjectivity that recalls the playtime of its own, that still remembers the wonderment and the joy of childhood. Such persons have the possibility of truly telling the story in a way in which the child will respond. The components of faith (belief in striving for the unknown), the embodiment of the story's meaning and the artistic expression reach the child who is still untouched by fragmented consciousness. Children can listen and relish with the attention that is paid to their own world of imaginary drama in everyday life. In this context, the world of religion is not something foreign to the young child. There is an integration and not an ambiguity. The daily life becomes religious and the religious becomes the daily life. The psychological, religious and intellectual development becomes a threefold development fostered by a community. The longterm appropriation in this case cannot be underestimated. The institutionalization of systematic decline has taken centuries to become emboned in humanity, its withdrawal could take just as long.

Such an exposition of biblical or religious stories may appear over dramatic. But if a Hamlet or a Caesar excites the minds and hearts of people everywhere and the quest is religious in its goal, why should the biblical narrative stand outside that excitement? We usually celebrate 'Good News'.

The brief outline of community growth enabling the emergence of what is technically called constitutive meaning is a long process. The fragmentation of western culture is massive and institutionalized. The culture is contributing to its own downfall by its very systems and ideology.[22] Eric Voegelin mentions that it takes 250 years to get rid of an idea.[23] If it takes that long to throw out the old it may take that long again to properly introduce the new.

The cultural content requires a shift in art, science, economics, politics and theology that reveals a shift in the notion of progress. Our prior analysis of the child's quest is not akin to any notion of progress that views psychology as an increase in the use of technological advances such as the computer.

The computer has taken on a more than vital role in current psychology and dissertation programmes. It might be exemplified in the following fashion. A child is presented the following puzzle.

The objective is to connect all dots with four straight lines without lifting the pen from the paper. The child will begin drawing lines in various directions, trying various combinations until he or she finally gets it. The computer, because of electric impulses, will try all the same wrong combinations only it will do it all in a few seconds. That is presently considered to be an intelligent advancement for humanity. The computer has no intelligence. The child gets the puzzle through the quest, trial and error and insight, in other words, through intelligence. The computer gets the answer by trial, error, rejection and finally conformity with the request of the original program. There is no pure desire by the computer. It is responding to electric impulses that initiate further activity. There is no insight. The computer will still have to do a similar thing the next time it is fed the same puzzle, the child will not. The drive for reliance on statistical law as a way of making and developing policies has made the computer popular in modern psychology. The quest of psychology requires further investigation into statistical law to properly understand its role in human living.[24] The child as quest is a search for meaning in a finite world. Meaning cannot move toward the Transcendent through the absence of the same in a computer. This type of shift in global psychology make take the 250 years of which Voegelin speaks. The problem may get so bad that it eventually invites solution.[25] But the basic orientation of this paper is towards a shift in religious educators that in the longterm will assist in a shift in community. In such a shift of meaning in psychology, the possibility of the emergence of foundational persons, to handle the task of educating children in the content of their faith, is greater. The culture becomes an orientation that mediates integration and not ambiguity or what we have called fragmented consciousness.

Our discussion of teachers as embodiments of religious meaning raises a further point, the notion of catechisms. It is apparent that any person off the street cannot teach religious education. In most religious education programs, it is presently carried out by persons ill-qualified for the task. We ask that a mathematics professor know mathematics, of a religious educator, we only ask that they love God, but what do they know about that love, its object, and the implications of both? The teacher's role requires centrally a grasp of contemporary authenticity. In such an area the catechism is not the primary focus. Addressing the question (child) and telling the story have no organizational structure per se. To introduce the catechism is to ignore the different questions of different children and an attempt to externally systematize intellectual, religious and psychological growth. A guideline totopics can be introduced, but if the topic is not relevant to a ten year old child, it is like speaking to an animal about the nature of thirst. A guideline of topics would have to be sensitive to the questions that arise. Such a program can only be formulated by those having expertise in the religious and methodological fields.

Our effort in this chapter has been to spell out some elements of reform that might aid in the shift of community to the proper reception of questions from any and all children. We have touched on many points and many specialized fields. The problems of art, science, economics, politics, and theology must be spelled out by the corresponding specialists. But their reorientation is required before they can address the problem as related to cultural crises. Common sense cannot head such a shift. It would seem to lie in the discovery of interiority and the guidance by such persons of the community. In the following chapter, we shall elaborate on an invariant basis, on which such specialization may begin the task of its own reorientation towards an integrated world of humankind that knowingly seeks God in any and all quests.

CHAPTER V

"An Invariant Basis"

In the preceding chapter, we spoke of the need for communal shift in order to help human beings grow authentically. We mentioned undifferentiated and differentiated consciousness as problem and solution, respectively, to the cultural crisis. It remains in this chapter to outline a structure that is transcultural, a basis for functional specialization and a mode of beginning the differentiation of consciousness.

Fr. Bernard Lonergan offers an analysis of the acts of consciousness by a turn to the subject.[1] One reflects on the acts or data of consciousness so as to give an account of its terms and relations. The task is one that the subject alone must carry out, for they are one's own operations. Any revision of the structure of experience, to question, to insight, to judgement, calls for a revision of the structure one used to arrive at the judgement of revision. In order to check out one's analysis one must first experience it, question it (What is it?), understand it and draw conclusions. A rejection of the former structure also rejects the latter structure.

A presentation of the structure for possible revision might be made in the following manner:

> Has anyone anywhere ever experienced anything?
>
> Has anyone anywhere ever asked a question about their experiences?
>
> Has anyone anywhere ever understood anything?
>
> Has anyone anywhere ever made a judgement about anything?

If any culture or individual can respond 'no' to any of the above questions, he or she or they, would then have to proceed to give an account of the process used to arrive at the judgement of 'no'. For 'no' is an answer to a question into experience that reveals some understanding of the question asked, even if that understanding is merely the meaning derived from early grammar lessons on the interrogative sentence. To disclaim doing any of the above is to be silent such as the dog that lays down in a disinterested fashion when the master asks the dog if it would like a rigorous expansion of its muscular compound.

The Chinese, Greek, Hebrew, Christian and atheist can all ask the above four questions.[2] Their replies will affirm the presence of such a structure of knowing. This structure not only underpins races and creeds but also the things people do such as; common sense, science, scholarship, interiority and theology.

But nevertheless, knowing this basis does not bring about a shift in the way people live. Living must be shaped and the dynamic structure for that shaping must rise from a basis that is authentically human. Reaping the benefits of such a dynamic structure calls for the implementation of such a discovery by the discoverers into the institutions that shape human living. And just as the structure of human consciousness is forever open to further questions, so the institutions and systems must portray that same open endedness.[3]

In the mid-sixties Lonergan finally arrived in his thinking at a method for theological collaboration. He set out eight functional specialities in part II of Method in Theology - research, interpretation, history, dialectic, foundations, doctrines, systematics and communications. These would not separate, but distinguish the labours of theologians. One person could no longer handle the entire task. The volume of contemporary scholarship was beyond one man's life's work. In short description, functional specialization operates as follows: one begins with gathering the data that is relevant: the data is interpreted: the historian ascertains what was going forward in such a period: dialecticians settle on the opposing views of historians: foundations determine which views are the positions that proceed from the presence of intellectual, moral and religious conversion: doctrines are reached by the application of a method that distinguishes functional specialities and uses the functional specialty foundations to select doctrines among the multiple choices presented by the functional specialty dialectics; systematics promotes an understanding of the realities affirmed in doctrines, and communications has the task of communicating to the faithful the results of the other seven specialities. When new questions and/or new data arise, the process begins again. It is open-ended, constantly returning to a new beginning, ever seeking a better understanding of its operations and its work.

Just as the terms and relations of the structure of human consciousness are subject to further clarification, so will any method be subject to that same expansion. For the future will raise further relevant questions.[4] In strange fact, being faithful includes the hope that man will ask further relevant questions in order that living becomes more humane, more authentic, i.e. closer to the divine plan.

Lonergan's method is an attempt to provide for the theologian a complementary structure, grounded by the acts of human sensitive consciousness from below and by moral and religious conversion from above. This method, through all seven functional specialities and finally fhrough communications, would reveal to humankind an authentic theology of praxis, one that addresses human authenticity, human livability and human survival. This enrichment calls for an intellectual conversion for everyone in any of the eight specialities and a moral and religious conversion in the last five. The first three can be carried out by an atheist to the extent that one is merely gathering data, interpreting it and forming a historical perspective. To go beyond this raises the question of value and judgement. The dialectician must know the difference between satisfaction and value if he is to have any possibility of certitude in decisions of the Christian world.[5]

Lonergan's method is a means of reorientating society for the faithful. But the dynamics of human consciousness also theorizes about economics and politics. These areas are affecting the tension and hopes of many people the world over. Just as our theological method is a structure build upon the operative minds of theologians and historians, so must our economic and political theories show that same foundation. Economic theory that enhances human livability may be characterized by the following quotation:

"The emergent standard of living is an aggregate of rates at which goods and services pass from the productive process into the standard of living."[6] At present, economic theory would seem to be the opposite of this, therefore the standard of living is being dictated in the west by the policies of multi-nationals whose prime objective is mass consumption and profit maximization.

Regarding political theory, Fred Lawrence writes: "In relation to the structure of the human good that constitutes the form of any society the question, What's the story? becomes especially pertinent as we shift our attention from the level of (the terms and relations of) the good of order to that of terminal values."[7] Later in this same work, Lawrence traces the history of contemporary western political structures. Lawrence locates its origin in the 15th chapter of The Prince by Machiavelli.

"...Many have imagined republics and principalities which have never been seen or known to exist in reality: for how we live is so far removed from how we ought to live, that he who abandons what is done for what ought to be done will rather learn to bring about his own ruin than his preservation. A man who wishes to makea profession of goodness in everything must necessarily come to grief among so many who are not good. Therefore it is necessary for a prince who wishes to maintain himself to learn how not to be good, and to use this knowledge and not use it according to the necessity of the case."[8]

"...The trajectory of political thought stretching in one wave from Machiavelli through Hobbes, Locke, Smith and in a second wave from Rousseau through Kant, Hegel, and Marx is rooted in the Machiavellian option to, in Lonergan's formulation, "develop 'realist' views in which theory is adjusted to practice and practice means whatever happens to be done."[9]

In this manner, practice precedes theory and because of practice's lack of the latter, practice is awry and theory cannot escape its direction unless theory takes on a turn to terminal value. This problem of theory and practice is present in western universities, in their departments, in their administration and in their expansion. The need for reorientation requires an invariant basis that seeks value in the theoretic and the practical. The basis offered here is the analysis of human consciousness as a structure that drives for value and is the source of originating value that is utilized in the practical affairs of human living.

Just as the possibilities for economic and political theory emerge through an analysis and knowledge of human authenticity, so theology takes its stand on the same basis. "The basic idea of the method we are trying to develop takes its stand on discovering what human authenticity is."[10]

Our digression to political and economical theory is to show the need for a shift to an analysis of the data of consciousness to develop a notion of what human authenticity is. The data, or acts of consciousness, underpin all human activity. Therefore, if society is to be authentic, all human activity must be an outgrowth of an appreciation of human authenticity. No system or institution can claim immunity from the value sought by intellectual consciousness.

In Second Collection, Lonergan defines authenticity as that species which would reach for a "contemporary, concrete, dynamic, maximal view that endeavors to envisage the range of human potentiality and to distinguish authentic from unauthentic realization of that potentiality."[11]

McShane explains authenticity in a view perhaps more amicable to the lone subject; "It is for each one to answer out of the contingencies of one's nerves and years, one's bread and butter, one's hopes, one's loves, one's fears, within the concrete mesh of the universe's needs."[12]

McShane goes on to speak of the pathos of Wonder in terms of discovering and rediscovering oneself. I would relate this wonder back to chapter two, the wonder of the child exemplified in dramatic playtime and objectified in the question for intelligence. This wonder as authentic is the natural desire to know blossoming in its potentialities. The nurturing of that wonder can bring forth schemes of recurrence and emergence that will accelerate the growth of the subject and the culture, intellectually, morally and religiously. It is to this wonder and pattern of human consciousness that a method in theology must address itself. This manner of addressing the institutions, systems, and art that emerge in a society, will find its basis in the authentic subject. The architecture will not dwarf the person but praise their humanness, their creativity, their intelligence, their love of God.

Education centres and programs will be places of familiarity regarding the 'at-homeness' and atmosphere for growth and joy. The teacher in love with the child's quest, God, combined with the knowledge that the child is a quest, will enrich the child's wonderment and experience of the love of God flowing in the hearts of those they live and learn with. Discipline problems (as the questing child has been mistakenly called) may take a backseat and be replaced by the growing question everseeking new things and new dreams and uncovering new mysteries of life. It is an envisagement of community life that springs from self-discovery that can only be made actual through humanity's preparedness to work in the complementarity that method in theology demands of the single subject.

"It may be that inner religious and outer socio-cultural factors come together to constitute a new religious consciousness inasmuch as (1) the inner religious factor resembles an intra structure which (2) the outer socio-cultural factor makes possible, or begins to countenance, or expresses, or interprets the religious experience."[13]

One could go on to indicate the efforts of scholars to delineate certain features of this thesis. My purpose was not such exposition, but to draw on more central work, mainly Lonergan's analysis of the cognitive acts of human consciousness, in an attempt to reveal the implications it has for methodical education, more specifically religious education. But our point in chapter two regarding the question as religious, reveals the Genesis point, <u>all</u> is <u>of</u> God, all is revealing God to humanity. The intelligibilities imminent in scientific data are not accidents.[14] The social sciences will have to look to the data of the growing consciousness for their proper field of study. It is a new view of life and living. But it is the education of children in such a manner that will reveal the truths and shortcomings of present work to future generations. The present culture is not equipped to criticize a stage of meaning that it itself has not arrived at, developmentally speaking.

"That shift has been our topic all along, but particularly, the shift as it must needs occur in the institutions of higher leaning. Who is to educate the educators of educators - and of managers, lawyers, politicians, doctors, presidents, party-secretaries."[15]

This is as much a 'criticism' of the present dilemna, as it is a 'statement' on the way things are now and the need for a change, for a turn to value, a turn to the possibilities of human joy. Those possibilities can be experienced, in the full and free wonder of the child seeking out its world, its quest, to 'see' beyond.

CHAPTER VI

"Practicality of Method"

When I speak of practice I do not wish to infer how one can use audio-aids, etc. in order to raise a particular question or move a student to a possible and perhaps particular insight. These aids can assist if used properly and if films, music, slides, etc. are designed to achieve such, but these aids can only be factual (nominal knowledge) or experimental.[1] In both cases there is required a 'going beyond' that does not often occur in the student because the aid itself is inadequate, or more precisely, 'going beyond' is not cultivated adequately and heuristically.

In Chapter two we hinted at a dialogue and a relationship between teacher and student.[2] Questions seek out a dialogue between people. When a child's questions are responded to correctly[3] by another (i.e. teacher, parent, friend) there is a sign of concern[4] for that child's inquiry. 'This person who helps me somehow loves me.' If the teacher considers the questions irrelevant or stupid, children withdraw. This child may feel embarrassed, or come to believe they are stupid. Once their questions stop, so does their attention shift, they seek out a world where they find response. It may be in peer groups or it may be in the world of imagination or artistry where they can resume some autonomy. This is not to say imagination or artistry are negative activities, but a complete withdrawal can harm the full development of the child. There is a need to integrate such activities with the dialogue of the classroom. The autonomy achieved through such activities exists for the child because the child can and will answer his or her own questions, correctly or incorrectly. The dialogue becomes a personal conversation with oneself. It is still an autonomy that seeks help, that seeks answers but lacks the heuristic dialogue of new questions and new insights into situations. One may be awry and fall into a deeper neurosis.[5]

A negative response to questions can make the child feel unloved. 'Why are my questions not important enough to answer? These are my questions - of me.' These remarks may not be as conscious as we make them out to be but the child is slowly scarred until eventually the society is unable to cure the hurts and one ends up with what we call a criminal or 'nutcase'. In both cases it began a long time ago and the evil was not of the child.

In the past and in the present, we have adverted to content, as priority, to the extent that the act of question itself has no relevance. The content becomes so important that any child's questions that appear slightly off the topic are ignored or put off to a later date, too late in most cases for the child. If a child is way off the topic, it is for a reason and is a sign to the teacher that some personal dialogue is in order in such a case.

There is required a nurturing of the child's questing to help them make their own judgements and not deprive them of their own ability as transcendent subjects. Through this process, the child is slowly able to discern the difference between progress and decline on their own.[6] That is the process of maturation, becoming an adult. Such discernment presupposes understanding and the ability to make rational judgements. Such conscious acts are not fully developed for young children. They are still seeking understanding and judgements are not complete as yet. 'Why is it so?' is only occasionally raised.

Children do not actually know why something might be evil or good. Some work this out alone in later years. Because of this, punishment is a questionable activity in society that may have nothing to do with the development of human beings. I once envisaged a society where homes were designed and furnished more for children than for adults, or at least a happy compromise. How less often would the young child be getting into so much 'mischief'? This mischief as we call it is the quest of the child seeking to come to know his/her world. Is there innate evil in the child that seeks to disrupt one's home? The home seems presently built for adults and 'viewers', not for those infinite quests that explore the home as Columbus might have explored the New World. We have designed our world so that it puts children naturally in danger and then we punish them for something society set into motion a long time ago. It is leading the unexamined life that leads to such stupidities. If we love our children we could perhaps build a world that they would be safe in, feel loved in, wrapped in the arms of a loving world.

This brings us to the act of God's love. If God is the one unrestricted act of understanding then God understands children in their fullness. He loves children as they are and forgives in that same act of love. Children are called to respond to that love. They cannot understand morality but they can be called to respond to that love as they respond to a parent's love. Such reconciliation is the task of a good home, good liturgical practice, community life and a good education. Therefore there must be some signs of that child's life outside the liturgy in the liturgy. The unsafe world that we build for children is not a sign of the care and love we speak of in our liturgies. It is not God working through us. It is the unexamined life.

If the world were more of a child's world, the children would feel loved. Adults might laugh and play a little more often and make the community a more beautiful place, something akin to the world many of us remember as children or can see in the child as they play without purpose.

In the sixties, young people revolted against the cultural values sought by the west. Did governments, churches, people in general, address the questions of those people?[7] Why did such an event come about? Such questions never seemed to be asked seriously by the figures of authority in the various nations involved. All attempts were directed towards getting those people back into the 'stream of life'. Most of those people gave up and now wear three piece suits. Nothing changed. Their questions are still unanswered,conformity became their way of life. One might not condone their methods, but it was a sign of a valueless culture and a controlled culture that needed change. Lonergan points out the inadequacy of our present way of viewing the human subject in the following quotation:

> Many human scienties are trying to ride the bandwagon of the physicists and chemists, and a science of man is pursued as though man were just another electron or another atom. As long as human science is of that type, as long as it is carried out in that manner, we shall have creeping socialism.(8)

Addressing the questions of growing children, being open for new questions and new insights to add to the old as teachers, as parents, as leaders of the culture changes a culture into one that progresses or knows the difference between progress and decline. It seeks value in its politics, economics, religious rituals and playtime. In this manner, there is not rebellion later in life but a constant openness for growth. If we seek God, we can never be satisfied with any one point. God as beyond is always beyond leaving man always with room for growth, moving closer ever-seeking a new glimpse of the beatific vision, the building of the kingdom.

Children rebel quickly but not in a way that seems to threaten the culture at large, so we ignore the child's why's and what for's. Yet every child's question that asks 'why' questions the culture and if educators cannot offer an explanation of why such and such is so, the culture becomes superficial to the child and he or she opts for acceptance, escapism or rebellion. The culture must integrate its ritual, work and playtime so that ambiguity does not arise, the troubled consciousness we spoke of in chapter three. Each question of value that is unanswerable, questions the structure a culture is built upon. Is the culture seeking the human good, an outgrowth of human authenticity, intellectual, religious and moral conversion, or is it a game of hit and miss with no guidance but that of conformity with big names in history?[9] As we pointed out in chapter three, the big names have been mistaken more often than not. This conformity is under no universal law to yield to progress. The culture may be a product of decline.[10]

The practicality of the method proposed in this small book is not one that is implemented through committees and planning sessions.[11] The authenticity of a child is a growth process that grows naturally out of the pure desire to know. Its implementation is a massive project that calls for a new faculty psychology, a new view of life and being. It is a matter of letting children ask the questions that are theirs, that become theirs through the narrative and through answers to prior questions. Once children enter school, after already learning and practicing their native tongue without being asked to or advised on what the proper method is,[12] the same process can be carried on through school, experience to inquiry to judgement. Such a process occurs in mathematics, natural sciences, social sciences, economics, politics, theology - the directions of inquiry are characteristic of the question - unrestricted.

In practice, giving answers will not be helpful. The teacher must first of all present the experience to raise the question in the mind of the child and urge them on further through new experiences and questions to understand the original question and arrive at some conclusion on their own. Giving answers is a resortation to the nominalism discussed in chapter two. Understanding is part of the very texture of the child's being and as the insights accumulate they move to a coherent unity of a particular topic until the person can grasp the entirety of a particular field.[13]

A good example of the procedure from experience to question to insight is in Plato's dialogue where Socrates is discussing virtue with Menon.[14] In this discussion Socrates wishes to point out to Menon that knowledge is not given from one person to another, but that knowledge is somehow with each and everyone of us. Socrates speaks with a slave boy who understands little geometry and manages through diagram (visual experience) and question to bring the slave boy to a knowledge of the relationship between squares and the diagonals that cut across from one corner to the opposite corner of a square. The slave boy was eventually able to grasp it because Socrates presented the problem in the order of the way people come to know things. This practice makes the child feel at home while learning.

Teachers will have to understand the content of their lessons and present experiences that will raise the question in the child's mind. The teacher must then urge and nurture the child on to insight through love, affection, experience and question, never embarrassing or laughing at a question because a question is an act of intelligence. It would not arise if the child knew the answer. The child will eventually get the insight and formulate a judgement about the prior experience through the examples and nurturing of the teacher.

This book is entitled The Child as Quest. In chapter two we tried to point out the origin and goal of the quest itself. But it is the child's quest. Remove the quest completely from the child and you have a somambulist. Remove the quest to some large degree and youhave disinterestedness, boredom and passive acceptance of cultural norms. Show small concern for the quest and you have rebellion. Who is rebelling? Who is bored? Who is asleep? It is the child and yet it is the quest that has been altered. Therefore, I speak of the child as quest. The child may be disturbed by physical or chemical imbalances and we must leave that improvement to the medical faculty. But they too must come to grips with what they are trying to improve upon.

Three final points concerning the question remain

to be outlined. In the first place, questions are acts of intelligence; they are not the result of stupidity. Stupidity would yield no questions. All the questions that arise for the child in a particular field are relevant to their particular growth in that area. They need to understand what addition is before they can move on to multiplication. An insight into quantum physics without ever having done physics would possibly qualify as revelation.

Secondly, time is in some sense not as relevant as we today make it out to be. Programmes on television force feed high vomumes of nominal knowledge to their viewers. Little understanding takes place. It is merely a push for mass consumption, something like our current economic theory. Universities provide extensive books, readings, papers and exams for students. The students tend to become quite fearful of such procedures. There is excessive anxiety. Hospitals in university areas show high overdose rates in drug and alcohol just before and during examination periods.[15] There is a thrust to give the students as much as possible. What do they learn? How much time do they get to think? How many insights did you have in the last ten years and if you were 'unfortunate' enough to have attended a school of 'higher' learning, how many insights did you have while getting the degree?

Some students manage to grasp a fair amount in certain topics because they have had a background that for some reason nurtured them towards questioning and understanding. Those reasons are often negative; i.e. fear, peer pressure. Others memorize without understanding and get through. The last category maybe neurotic throughout the year and understand little of the subject. Questions and insights seldom come or occur when one is suffering from neurosis.[16] The urge to get through five courses in a three month semester at a present university and <u>learn</u> anything is, or should be, a joke. Universities are presently dominated by economic survival, or professional neurotic defense mechanisms. What should be taught or how it should be taught lacks an underlying foundation so the university plays the same hit and miss game that the culture as a whole is playing. A professor in one of my undergraduate classes once remarked in a lecture on "The Meaning of Higher Education" that if one wants an education, do not come to the university; just hang around the halls, get the names of all the big books from the professors and go home and read them! Because of the absence of insights in the university there is a high degree of truth to this statement. If one learns anything in the university, they have been lucky and probably had a professor who tried sometime in his or her life to understand understanding and remained alive. It takes time for the teacher to raise the proper question and even longer perhaps to nurture and bring forth the relevant insight as in Socrates' discussion with Menon, the slave boy. To put time limits on teaching and learning is to totally ignore the structure of intellect.

Finally, space, insights can take place anywhere. If we reflect on our own experiences of intelligence (and I hope we all will for that is the challenge set forth in chapter two), we have probably experienced it in the bath, walking, driving or flying. Questions and more particularly, insights are outside the restrictions of specific events which are tied to place and time. Insights occur without warning, perhaps when one least expects it. The current atmosphere of university classrooms and schools is not always condusive to creativity or intellectual development.[17]

Our initial effort has been the practicality of method. We have spoken of practice and of improper practice, its problems and results. It remains that the teacher must take up the task presented in chapter two of discovering the act of question in oneself and through insight come to know its relevance in teaching and learning. Method reveals its full fruits through effective meaning.[18] Both constitutive and effective meaning concern the living and practice of our cognitive achievements. They will only be as effective, in teaching, to the degree one has first of all worked out the cognitive meaning of question (intelligence) and secondly, to the degree they possess the meaning. Knowing of the question and its relevance is only the first step. Implementation consists of the embodiment of the same so that one lives by one's judgements and practices it in that living. It is a long and lonely sojourn that is offered but its fruits will be in the 'eyes' of the beholder, in the children's faces, lives and relationships as the quest remains alive, growing, everseeking new discoveries, new possibilities for human survival.

In summation, practice is a living experience out of an appropriation of "the intelligible unity-identity-whole genetically and dealectically integrative of the six-levelled events of the life of a man or a woman".[19]

> ...the range of human skills and techniques of economics and politics, of sciences and philosophies, of cultures and religions is diversified. Only the broadest set of concepts can provide the initial base and the field of differences that will be adequate to dealing with a variable set of moving systems that regard the universe of being.(20)

And underlying that broad set of concepts is the human subject involved subjectively as it is all he or she can do, in the stuff of life, the dancing, the planning, the working, the moulding, the deliberating about the future of a universe that is in one way ours and in another way it never will be ours, yet it beckons us on to understand all that there is to be understood.

> What I am continually stressing is the slow growth of the subject, of you and I, in Weltanschauung, in the self-appreciative, heuristic structure of our conscious intentionality, a structuring which, if authentic, mediates a transformation of the drama of our daily encounter in a manner compatible with our psychic potential.(21)

It is that authentic mediation transforming the drama of life that this chapter strives to bring home. Practice that will address the child authentically will come from the transformed authentic subject who mediates, who teaches and learns on a pivotal point of common ancestry, in its broadest meaning and common object in all Their mystery. (Trinity, three in one).

CHAPTER VII

Science and the Arts

Method as portrayed in this book and as you will hopefully find it active in yourself, is not restricted to religious education. As I pointed out in chapter four, in areas of economics and politics, it is the failure to advert to this structure or to human authenticity that has led humankind astray in devising structures for human livability.

Intellectual consciousness is utilized by mathematicians, geometers, architects, physicists, chemists, botanists, zoologists, philosophers, theologians, musicians, artists, historians, engineers, writers, economists and politicians. In some areas such as the last two, an insight may be occuring only every two or three hundred years.[1] In others, it may be daily. The point is that underlying scientific method and methodical scholarship is the person reading, experimenting, asking questions, getting insights, drawing conclusions. Questions, insights and judgements are not of a new nature of data. They are of the person who is awakened, through sensible data and the pure desire to know, to conscious inquiry. Data is a component of knowledge and reality, just as are question and insight. The three culminate in judgement, in knowledge, in reality.

In teaching science or the arts, the same structure is in process as it is in religious education. The same care in nurturing the student to insights is required. The problem that presently arises is the explanation scientists offer for scientific method.[2] The method as carried out does arrive at the discovery and formulation of laws in the various fields. There lie many problems in the area of objectivity and on notions of reality that have invaded all areas but especially the social sciences to the point that their empiricality is extremely restricted to an area of statistical observations and the particular insights such has to offer have only a minor bearing on the possibilities of an alive and vibrant consciousness.[3] There is the entire area of empirical consciousness which the psychologist and sociologist use to formulate data, experiments and conclusions yet refuse to consider empirical consciousness as data, therefore they find no invariant basis for humankind.

The structure of methodical science is not our initial purpose in this chapter but it bears relevancy to mention that no field of inquiry exists without an inquirer; the child, the adolescent, the adult.

All fields of inquiry must be taught in the early stages in a manner as outlined in chapter two. Once one has gained the initial insights and understood basic terminology, one can move along quicker and more independently.

By nurturing the quest from conception on through life in every aspect of life, both at home and in school and in play, the child grows with the integrated consciousness we spoke of in earlier chapters.

Science at present moves along in a vacuum. Value judgements have not been part of scientific discovery. It is discovery for discovery's sake in the name of progress. Is it so? arises, but on a different level of responsibility, these questions arise: Is this for the human good? Is this progress? Progress, again, is not defined by higher buildings and numerous committees to institutionalize; welcoming, home visitation, faster cars and faster computers. They are the products of a culture in decline. They arise from inauthenticity.

Authenticity, such as that of the African tribes do not have to form committees to make sure the sick and elderly are cared for. In some circles it means leaving the old behind. There were cultural traditions for the good of the whole. Is our present neglect of the sick and elderly good for the whole? Can we survive as a culture if we decide to love and care for those in need around us? Should we institutionalize the care of the old or sick? This may seem cruel to the medical profession but our emphasis in medicine on the physical well being has left the psyche in sad shape. It might be better to live a short happy life than a long bitter one providing the best possible care at home. These are questions for the community at large, the theologians, the scientists, the physicians. At present, psychiatric wards are doing a fine business and people talk about coping. Should we cope with decline, idiocy and inhumanity? We might say going crazy is escaping into reality from this unreality, this inhumane culture.

These are large points which call for great expansion and explanation. I hint at them here in a mocking fashion to expose the urgency in raising the question in you, the reader. If you sense inauthenticity, it then becomes the problem of survival, but its potentialities are so much more.

"Will they still need me
Will they still feed me
When I'm sixty-four?"[4]

That is our quest, to be alive when we are sixty-four, seventy-four, eighty-four and so on. To die psychically, before biological cessation prepares us for the resurrection, is an event we should mourn as much graver than the loneliness someone's resurrection can cause to us. I refer you back to our discussion of art in all its forms for one's release from the slow dying of our quest.

We may have appeared to have sidetracked to far away places, but never have we left the confines of our own heuristic structure, our mind, the topic at hand. At this point I might recall to you our initial quotation in the introduction by Blaise Pascal: "Wisdom leads us back to childhood. Except ye become as little children." Our emphasis has been on the first part of that statement. We have not ventured on an exgetical account of what Jesus or Matthew may have meant by the second part, but there are Christological and hermeneutical implications in our analysis of consciousness in that Jesus too was human.[5] It is hoped that the odd twist that I spoke of at the beginning is now more apparent and meaningful to you, the reader.

"And if this view of the book is considered far-out and far-fetched, perhaps it is because 99% of contemporary psychologists are paranoic, schizophrenic, anaesthetized, or truncated. For they too are part of our present time. Nor do I claim exemption."[6]

In my use of this quotation, I might add educators of religion, natural scientists, historians and economists. We learn only slowly to shed old habits and ours are as old as human beings. It is our history and it cannot become our future if we are to survive as vibrant quests in the universe of being.[7]

EPILOGUE

We have made little mention of appropriation and affirmation throughout this work although it has been hinted at continuously.[1] To discover the question in oneself is to affirm oneself as a questioner, and to bring it to the level of inhabiting one's way of teaching in its full implications, is to appropriate the act of question. This entire field has more than relevant implications for epistemology and metaphysis. Lonergan has worked this area out in its fuller ramifications in INSIGHT. When these areas come to life for the reader, the fuller integration and relevance of cognitional analysis may come to 'light' for the subject.

I have been grappling with Lonergan's 'enterprise'[2] for almost six years and I still feel my own personal inadequacy in regards to an authentic expression of who I am. Dr. Philip McShane has intimated in conversations with me and in print the immensity of Lonergan's Challenge and his (McShane) own personal struggle of reaching up to such a thinker as Lonergan. In the introduction to Language, Truth and Meaning, McShane speaks of Lonergan's own growth as 'slower than one might be inclined to assume'.[3] This is not an apology for my own inadequacy, there are many, it is an effort to converse with you the reader in a way that will blossom forth into new perspectives of human growth. The more one reflects on the immensity of the project the more 'long-term optimism' becomes a way of life. And that is what I am talking about all along a way of life and living and loving. This small book intimates a mistake in education that is supported by the culture as a whole. One cannot expect a closure of those doors over night. They are old and set hard in their places.

There are many running ahead and doing the work that is too much a product of our time. The authenticity of our culture has not yet reached the stage of growth required to handle projects without firmly established foundations to authenticate experience and allow the various categories of the heuristic structure to open up and provide the opportunity for the progressive nature of method to operate. It is building the roof of the home where there are no walls or basement foundations laid. The "ongoing collaboration' that was spoken of in 1970 at the International Lonergan Conference in Florida was a nice thought, it doesn't seem to fill the minds of too many of those who have carried on from the meeting 13 years ago. Academic polity is putting an extra burden on personal survival that I share little enthusiasm with nor do I wish to contribute to what might be revealing itself as a repetition of Scotus' treatment of Aquinas in the late 13th century and such a repetition we can afford only at the expense of immense human suffering.

I turn now to Philip McShane, whom I quote endlessly in his ability to provide the data which helps me understand, for a final remark on human growth toward possible joy.

"...in so far as one has really spoken, flowed forth in word and gesture, one has data through which, by dedicated contemplative reflection, one may glimpse what occurs in God. There is speech in God, in an ambience of Unrestricted Understanding. That speech is not about God: it is God, a single raptuous Word. Again, in so far as one has listened, not merely with ear but with understanding eye and heart and toe muscle, then one may reflectively move to some glimpse of that absorbent Joyous Ear of God which is the Spirit."[4]

The Unrestricted act is man's quest in each utterance. It is beyond the circuits of computers. It is the long rollingsea touching horizons drawing one's contemplation to a moment of bliss, to touch that secret where sky meets ocean, where eternity blesses its own presence and refurbishes the empty rooms of one's contemplative soul: that quest to understand God.

NOTES

INTRODUCTION

1. Pascal, B., *Pascal Pensees*, Tr. by A.J. Krailsheimer, Penguin Books, Great Britain, 1966, p. 51.
2. *The Jerusalem Bible*, Editor, A. Jones, Doubleday & Co., N.Y. 1966, Matthew 18: 1-5.
3. Pascal, p. 51.
4. Ibid.
5. Lonergan, B.J.F., *Method in Theology*, Darton Longman & Todd, London, 1973, p. 55.
6. McShane, P., *Lonergan's Challenge to the University and Economics*, University of America Press, 1980, p. 91.

CHAPTER I

1. McShane, Philip, *The Shaping of Foundations: Being at Home in the Transcendental Method*, University Press of America, 1976, p. 8.
2. Carter, G. Emmett, *The Modern Challenge to Religious Education*, William H. Sadler, Inc., N.Y., Chicago, 1961, p. 74.
3. Carter, *op. cit.*, p. 75.
4. Carter, p. 78
5. Carter, p. 80.
6. Carter, p. 81.
7. Carter, p. 85.
8. Carter, p. 81.
9. *New Catechetical Methods*, ed. by J. Goldbrunner, tr. by Sr. M. Veronica Riedl, O.S.F., "Catechesis and Encounter" by J. Goldbrunner, University of Notre Dame Press, 1965, p. 17.
10. Carter, p. 82
11. Carter, p. 84.
12. Carter, p. 83.
13. A close study revelas a lack of any proper hermeneutics regarding the biblical content. Also a neglect of the maturation process of children to morality or value judgement is evident in the effort to seek *all* truths in the bible. See Section 8 of junior program of David C. Cook material.
14. Carter, p. 89
15. Carter, p. 89.
16. Carter, p. 271.

17. Councils of Baltimore. Final council in 1884 delegated to a commission the task of preparing a Catechism for Christian Doctrine which appeared for the cleric in 1885.
18. Lonergan, B.J.F., A Second Collection, ed. by W.J. Ryan and B.J. Tyrrell, Westminister Press, 1974, p. 160.
19. McShane, P., Music That is Soundless: An Introduction to God for the Graduate, University Press of America, 1977, Appendix p. 83.
20. Lonergan, B., Method in Theology, Darton Longman & Todd, London, 1973, 2nd Edition, p. XI.
21. Lonergan, op. cit., p. 55.
22. Lonergan, B., Insight: A Study of Human Understanding, Darton, Longman & Todd, 1957, Chapter I, Section 2.4.

CHAPTER II

1. Lonergan, Insight, p. 5-6
2. Ibid., p. 9.
3. Ibid., Chapter XVIII.
4. Ibid., Chapter I, Section 2.
5. McShane, Music That is Soundless, op. cit., p. 30-31.
6. Lonergan, Method in Theology, Chapter 1, See also Insight Chapter XIX, Section 1, 2 & 3.
7. McShane, Lonergan's Challenge to the University and the Economy, University Press of America, 1980. The Shaping of Foundations: Being at Home in the Transcendental Method, University Press of America, 1976. Dr. McShane attempts to illustrate the actual process of methodical science in various fields through the two above works.
8. The New American Bible, Catholic Biblical Association of America, Thomas Nelson Publishers, N.Y., 1971, Genesis 1.1.
9. McShane, The Shaping of Foundations, op. cit., Introduction, p. vi - viii.
10. McShane, Music That is Soundless, p. 2.
11. Van der Post, L., The Dark Eye of Africa, William Norman & Co., N.Y., 1955, Introduction, p. 16.
12. Voegelin, E., The Ecumenic Age, Louisiana State University Press, 1974, Introduction.
13. This refers to the child's single development as an instance of man's entire historical conscious development. Refer to McShane, Randomness, Statistics & Emergence, Gill & MacMillan, Dublin, 1970, Chapter 1, p.40ff.

14. Hesse, Hermann, The Journey to the East, London, 1970, p. 12.
15. McShane, Music That is Soundless, p. 18.

CHAPTER III

1. Lonergan, A Second Collection, op cit., p. 269, Insight was written from a moving viewpoint whereupon various exercises are to be carried out by the reader. In this way the book, Insight, is one which guides one to an analysis of the data of consciousness culminating in a theory of metaphysics and affirmation of God.
2. Lonergan, Method in Theology, p. 84.
3. Ibid., p. 84
4. Lonergan, Insight, p. 582 - 2.
5. Introduction to Psychology, Morgan/King, McGraw, 1966, p. 454.
6. Lonergan, B., Verbum: Word and Idea in Aquinas, ed. D. Burrell, University of Notre Dame Press, 1967, p. 25.
7. Ibid., p. 25
8. Ibid., p. 25, n. 122.
9. Kant, I., Critique of Pure Reason, tr. by F. Max Muller, Anchor Books, N.Y., 1966, Section 1, First Division, Transcendental Analtic, Chapter 2, p. 100 - 106. See also Lonergan, Verbum, p. 25.
10. Collins, James, A History of Modern European Philosophy, Bruce Publishing Co., U.S.A., 1954, p. 624.
11. The development of existentialism was an effort tocombat the extreme Idealism of the German tradition rooted in Hegel. Kierkegaard began this emphasis by a turn to the subject. It moved through Nietzsche, Jaspers,Marcel, Camus and Satre. Many of the Phenomenologists such as Merleau-Ponty have often been described as existentialists. Their emphasis have been more on epistemological systems. European existentialism has never culminated into a complete Christian Philosophical system. Many of the existentialists such as Satre claimed to be atheists. Lonergan's turn to the subject depicted in Insight a record of his own analysis of cognition which he then develops and expands into an epistemology, a metaphysics and in chapter XIX, an affirmation of God.
12. Babin, Pierre, Methods: Approaches for the Catechesis of Adolescents, tr. by John F. Murphy, Herder & Herder, N.Y., 1967, p. 104 - 107.
13. Lonergan, Insight, p. 9, 191-205.

14. McShane, Music That is Soundless.
15. Lonergan, Method in Theology, p. 55.
16. Lonergan, A Second Collection, p. 8.

CHAPTER IV

1. McShane, P., "Middle Kingdon: Middle Man", Unpublished paper presented at the Lonergan Conference in Boston, June 1981, p. 4.
2. Lonergan, Insight, p. 175 - 181.
3. Snell, Bruno, The Discovery of Mind, Harper Torchbooks, N.Y., 1960, Chapter 1, 3, 5, 9.
4. Lonergan, Method in Theology, p. 84.
5. Ibid., p. 272.
6. Van der Post, L., op. cit., Introduction.
7. Ibid., Introduction.
8. Lonergan, Method in Theology, p. 84.
9. Butterfield, H., The Origins of Modern Science: 1300 - 1800, 2nd Edition, N.Y., 1966, p. 7.
10. Lonergan, Insight, p. 175 - 181.
11. Lonergan, Method in Theology, p. 107.
12. Ibid., p. 84.
13. The problem is solved for the methodologist in-as-much as he has understood the implications of the third stage of meaning.
14. Langer, S., Feeling and Form, Charles Scribner & Sons, 1953, p. 40.
15. Lonergan, Method in Theology, p. 64.
16. Ibid., p. 303-4.
17. Snell, B., op. cit., Chapters 3 & 5.
18. The structure and content of knowing and knowledge are an inseparable unity. McShane, Wealth of Self and Wealth of Nations, Exposition Press, N.Y., 1975, Chapters 1-5. Lonergan, Insight, Chapter X.
19. This orientation is to the child's growth as indicated in chapter 2, above.
20. Chapter 2 above, narrative and pure desire.
21. Chapter 2, above p. 11.
22. Lonergan, Method in Theology, p. 55.
23. Conversations with E. Voegelin at the Thomas More Institute, Thomas More Institute Papers, Montreal, 1976, p. 19.
24. Lonergan, Insight, Chapters 3 & 4.
25. Upon our present view of policy-making, things may get so bad, we admit we are doing nothing to help the situation, therefore, we turn about and seek an entirely new way. It may be years or centuries before this occurs.

CHAPTER V

1. Lonergan, Insight, Chapter 1 to 10.
2. Crowe, F.E., "Neither Jew nor Greek, but one Human Nature and Operation in All", Phillippine Studies (13), 1965.
3. Lonergan, Method in Theology, Chapter 5.
4. As indicated in Chapter 2, the meaning of particular terms and relations will bring forth further questions to be answered. The process would seem to be ongoing.
5. Lonergan, Method in Theology, p. 242.
6. McShane, Lonergan's Challenge, p. 119.
7. Lawrence, Fred, Lonergan Workshop Papers, Vol. 1, Scholars Press, Montana, 1978, p. 225.
8. Machiavelli, The Prince, Chaucer Press, Great Britain, 1975, p. 90-1.
9. Lonergan, Collection, ed. F. Crowe, Herder & Herder, N.Y., 1967, p. 116.
10. Method in Theology, p. 254.
11. A Second Collection, p. 165.
12. The Shaping of Foundations, p. 123-4.
13. "Prolegomena to the Study of the Emerging Religious Consciousness of our time", paper given by Lonergan at a Conference on Structuralism and Hermeneutics: Merging Horizons, held at York University, Toronto, November 1978.
14. Insight, Chapters 2, 3, 4.
15. Lonergan's Challenge, p. 84-85.

CHAPTER VI

1. Insight, p. 150, 322, 331.
2. Education might be viewed as an ongoing conversation between teacher and student or any two people. One presents the experience, the other receives it, strives to understand the data given and responds with some conclusion which becomes an experience for the first speaker.
3. Chapter 2, explanation and nurture.
4. Crowe, F.E., S.J., "Complacency and Concern in the Writings of Aquinas", Theological Studies (20), 1959.
5. Insight, p. 191. Although we are concerned more with preventing suppression of the pure desire, once one has become neurotic, rescue becomes a task for the analyst. See also R. Doran, "Dramatic Artistry", Lonergan Workshop papers ed. by Fred Lawrence, vol. 2, Scholars Press, 1981, p.165.

6. Method in Theology, Ch. 2, Sect. 7, Collection, ed. by F. E. Crowe, Palm Publishers, Montreal, 1967, Ch. 2 on hierarchic levels of more essential and more excellent ends.
7. Chomsky, Noam, American Power and the New Mandarins, Vintage Books, N.Y., 1969, Ch. 6, 7 and 8 for discussion of the problem. For an appreciation of the source of such a problem and failure for contemporary schemes to meet such problems, refer to Method in Theology, Ch. 2, Sect. 6 and 7.
8. Elizabeth & Mark Morelli, Understanding and Being, The Edwin Mellen Press, N.Y., 1980, Ch. 1.
9. Method in Theology, Ch. 2, Sect. 3 & 4.
10. Ibid., p. 55.
11. Ibid., p. 318.
12. Ibid., p. 27ff, p. 70-73.
13. Insight, p. 444 ff.
14. Great Dialogues of Plato, tr. by W.H.D. Rouse, ed. by Eric H. Warmington & P.G. Rouse, New American Library, N.Y., 1956, p. 43-49.
15. Technicians working regular night shifts in Hospital laboratories report an increase in alcohol and drug overdoses during examination time at nearby universities.
16. Insight, p. 191.
17. Langer, S., Feeling and Form, Charles Scribners Press, N.Y., 1953, p. 401.
18. Method in Theology, p. 362.
19. McShane, The Shaping of Foundations, p. 120.
20. Insight, p. 509.
21. The Shaping of Foundations, p. 13.

CHAPTER VII

1. Lonergan's Challenge, Ch. 6, more pointedly p. 109-110.
2. Insight, p. 423-430.
3. McShane, P., Randomness, Statistics and Emergence, Gill & MacMillan, Dublin, 1970, Ch. 5.
4. Sgt. Pepper's Lonely Hearts Club Band Album, The Beatles.
5. Lonergan, B.J.F., De Constitutione Christi, Gregorian Press, Rome, 1961. Also see Lonergan, Collection, ed. by. F.E. Crowe, Palm Pub., Montreal, 1967, Ch. 11, "Christ as Subject: A Reply".
6. Lonergan's Challenge, p. ix.
7. Insight, Ch. XII

EPILOGUE

1. _Insight_ on Affirmation, Ch. XI. On appropriation, Morelli & Morelli, _Understanding and Being_, Ch. 1.
2. Crowe, F.E., S.J., _The Lonergan Enterprise_, Cowley Pub. U.S.A., 1980. Fr. Crowe describes Lonergan's efforts and contribution as an Organon in our Times.
3. _Language, Truth and Meaning_, ed. by P. McShane, University of Notre Dame Press, 1972, Intro. by McShane, p. 2.
4. _Music That is Soundless_, p. ix.

ABOUT THE AUTHOR

After ten years in the public and private sector of employment, Mr. Henman returned to university and completed undergraduate studies in history and philosophy at Mount Saint Vincent University, Halifax, in 1979.

In 1982, he received a Master's in Theological Studies from the Atlantic School of Theology in Halifax. He has studied in Indiana, Boston and Montreal in the areas of philosophy, liturgy and Christology. He has also studied extensively with Dr. Philip McShane, widely regarded as one of today's leading authorities on the writings of Bernard Lonergan. Mr. Henman's first work is an extension of his graduate thesis. He is presently living in Halifax, Nova Scotia, with his wife and two children. He is Director of a Religious Education programme in the Archdiocese of Halifax.